WILLIAM
GAINES

MAD Man

Steven Otfinoski

ROURKE ENTERPRISES,INC.
VERO BEACH, FLORIDA 32964

Publisher's Note:
The publisher would like to thank Anne Gaines and the staff of MAD magazine for their valuable help and generous cooperation in putting this book together. Thanks also to Wendy Bucci, who graciously allowed us to use material from *Tales from the Crypt* in the preparation of this project.

A Blackbirch Graphics book.

Library of Congress Cataloging-in-Publication Data

Otfinoski, Steven.
   William Gaines / by Steven Otfinoski.
      p.   cm. — (Made in America)
   Summary: Chronicles the life of the madcap founder of the popular humor magazine which featured the motto "What—Me Worry?" and a character named Alfred E. Neuman.
   ISBN 0-86592-080-X
   1. Comic books, strips, etc.—United States—history and criticism—Juvenile literature. 2. Gaines, William M.—Juvenile literature. 3. Publishers and publishing—Juvenile literature. [1. Gaines, William M. 2. Publishers and publishing.] I. Title. II. Series.
PN6725.08 1993
070.5'092—dc20
[B]   93-16177
                                     CIP
                                     AC

Contents

What—Me Worry?

*"My staff and contributors
create the magazine.
What I create is the
atmosphere."*

On June 10, 1992, *MAD*
magazine ran a full-page message in *The
New York Times* newspaper. This was rather
remarkable because the magazine had
always maintained a low profile. But then
this was no ordinary message. It featured
a full-page portrait of *MAD*'s famous trademark, that freckled-faced, gap-toothed kid,
Alfred E. Neuman. Above the wide, familiar
grin, a single tear dripped from one eye.
Under the picture, the message's closing
words read:

"We'll miss you, Bill.
    Love,
       the Usual Gang of Idiots"

**Opposite: Bill Gaines was the funloving genius who
founded one of the most popular "comic" magazines in
America.**

The event that led to this rare show of
sentiment was the death, on June 3, 1992,
of William M. Gaines, 70, the man who had
run *MAD* since its birth. Bill's unique and
wild sense of humor—and his ability to run
a business—had turned *MAD* into one of
the greatest success stories in American
publishing. "My staff and contributors
create the magazine," he used to say
proudly. "What I create is the atmosphere."

Bill's Father Has a Brainstorm

Bill Gaines's motto for the first 25 years of
his life might well have been Alfred E.
Neuman's "What—Me Worry?" As a youth,
Bill left the worrying to others, mainly to
his go-getter father, Max. Originally an
elementary school principal, Max Gaines
left the school system to make big money
as a salesperson. But selling anything was
hard in the Great Depression of the 1930s.

Then one day Max started looking
through the attic of his Bronx, New York,
apartment. He came across some old comic
strips from the Sunday newspaper and re-
read them. Suddenly, he had a brainstorm.
What if he could reprint these old funnies
in book form and sell them? Would other
people enjoy reading them, too?

Bill's parents, Max and Jessie Gaines, pose for a portrait in the garden of their home in White Plains, New York, in 1945.

He took his idea to Eastern Color Printing, a company that had had a similar idea. But Eastern's reprints were as big as the newspapers they had originally appeared in. Max got the company to reduce the size of the reprints so they would be suitable for use in books. Under his guidance, Eastern published thousands of these books of Sunday funnies, which it gave away to various companies that sold candy, soft drinks, and other popular products that children usually bought.

The program was so successful that Max decided to try selling the books directly to the public. In May of 1934, the first issue of *Famous Funnies* hit the newsstands with the cover price of a dime. The comic book was born.

The growing numbers of comic-book readers soon tired of the old "Dick Tracy" and "Little Orphan Annie" reprints. As a result, new characters were created just for comic books. The most famous of the new characters was Superman. Max helped to sell the Superman character to Detective Comics (DC), also a publisher of comics.

For a time, Max worked with another publisher on a line of superhero comic books, including *The Flash* and *The Mighty*

Atom. But in 1945 he sold his share of the business and started his own line. Max was aware that as comic books were becoming big business, they were gaining the unfavorable attention of those who didn't like children reading such "trash." Max's new comics would be above such criticism. He called his company Educational Comics (EC) and set about retelling stories from history, science, and the Bible in comic-book format.

A Disappointing Son

Bill Gaines was born in New York City in 1922. He was the exact opposite of his hardworking father. Even Bill described himself as "a behavior problem" and "a difficult child." Max was bitterly disappointed in his only son and was convinced that Bill would never amount to anything. Bill seemed determined to prove his father right. He cared little about school, he seemed to have little or no ambition, and he was awkward and nonathletic. His main interest in life was performing practical jokes on his friends. After finishing high school, Bill went to the Polytechnic Institute of Brooklyn. He started out as a chemistry major but dropped out in his junior year.

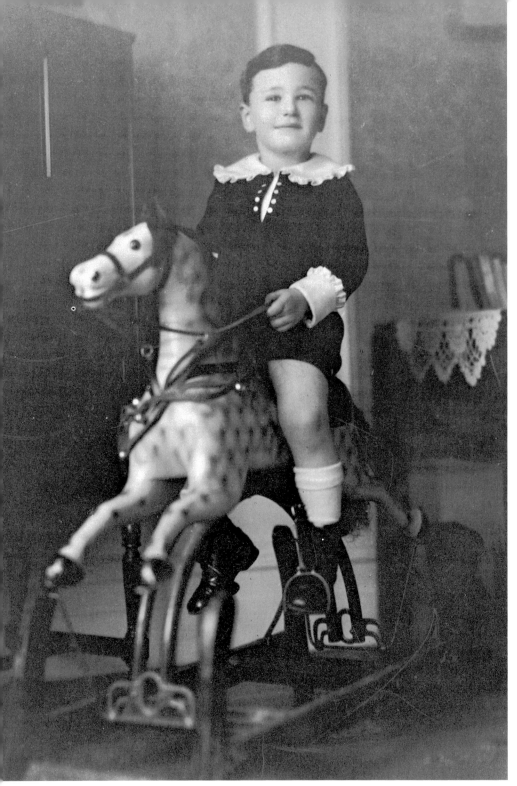

Bill Gaines, age 3.

Knowing that his father would be angry, Bill told him that he had left college because he had been drafted. Then he quickly joined the army. During his three years in the army, Bill married his second cousin, Hazel Grieb, with strong encouragement from his mother, Jessie.

After he left the army, Bill decided to follow in his father's footsteps and become a teacher. He enrolled in New York University. Then two major events occurred that

Bill, age 7, with his father and sister Elaine.

Bill dropped out of college to join the army. Here, he is shown in uniform, 1942.

turned Bill's life around—his wife left him, and his father died.

One day in 1947, Max Gaines was boating with a friend and his friend's son on Lake Placid in upstate New York. They were struck by another boat. Max managed to throw his friend's son to safety, but the two men died.

After Bill graduated from New York Unversity in 1948, his mother asked him to take over the family business, EC Comics. Even though the comic-book industry was booming, EC was $100,000 in debt. Educational Comics had a limited appeal to the average young reader.

At first, Bill didn't want to take over the failing business, but he finally agreed to do so. "I got the feeling that Bill went into the business as a joke, to see if he could screw up things, change them for his private amusement, and still manage to make money doing it...." said an old friend at DC Comics.

Bill did manage to have a lot of fun and make a lot of money, too. At last it seemed that the awkward young man had finally found something that made him happy. In the process, however, he made EC Comics into something that many people thought would have caused his poor father to turn over in his grave.

Horror, Thrills, and Laughs

By 1951, Bill was putting out nine comic books that were among the most popular in America.

Bill Gaines knew that to sell comic books you had to, above all, entertain your readers. So, out went the bible stories and the "E" in EC no longer stood for "Educational," but for "Entertaining." Like other forms of entertainment, comic books went through popular trends. The hottest trends in the post-World War II years were westerns, crime stories, and romances. Bill hired a talented comic-book artist named Al Feldstein. Together the two men prepared six new comic books for EC, with such titles as *Modern Love, Saddle Justice,* and *Saddle Romances*.

The First Horror Comics

EC's new comics were better received by the public, but Bill felt that they needed to be more interesting and exciting. He wanted to start a new trend. To his delight he discovered that Al Feldstein shared his love of suspense and horror. Bill and Al were both

In the 1950s, Bill teamed up with comic-book artist Al Feldstein and created a unique line of horror comics.

big fans of suspense radio programs, like "Lights Out" and "Inner Sanctum." These programs were known for their creepy hosts, who regularly introduced each week's shocking tale.

Bill and Al decided to try the same dark and creepy format in comic books. Their new comics, *The Vault of Horror* and *Tales from the Crypt*, based some of their stories on forgotten horror paperbacks of the 1920s and 1930s. Each story was introduced by two ghoulish characters called, appropriately enough, the Crypt-Keeper and the Vault-Keeper. The results, which were something new and original and very scary, became known as horror comics.

EC's horror comics were more than simple blood and gore. Bill hired the best writers and artists in the business to make his stories outstanding. The artwork was very well done, and the stories always ended with an unexpected twist. The stories had plenty of humor, too, with titles such as "Coffin Spell" and "Ooze in the Cellar."

And at times the horror had a purpose far beyond mere thrills. Bill and Al would sneak in stories that dealt with important issues of the day. This was a daring thing to do in the play-it-safe 1950s.

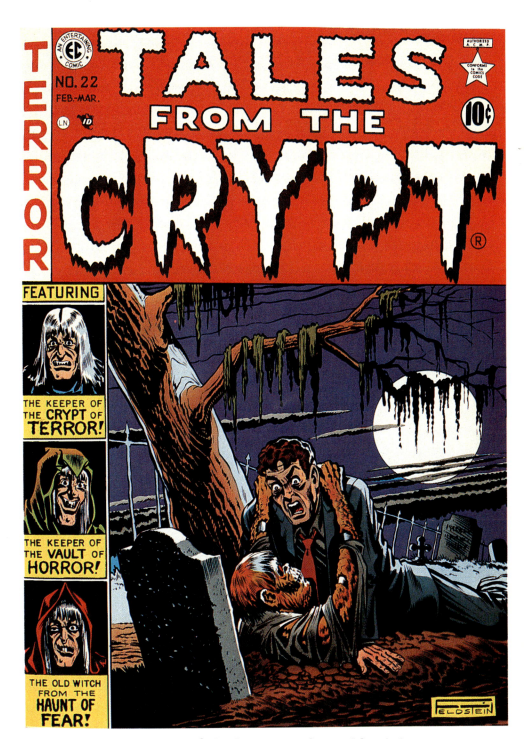

EC's new concept of the horror comic combined the best elements of humor, suspense, gore, and illustrations.

Sci-Fi and War

Another passion of Bill's was science fiction. Soon, EC's horror comics were joined by *Weird Science* and *Weird Fantasy*, as well as such new and original crime comics as *Shock SuspenStories* and *Crime Suspen-Stories*. The inspiration of the sci-fi comics was again the forgotten paperbacks of the 1920s and 1930s. Some of these previously published stories represented the finest science fiction of their day. Among EC's best work was a series of adaptations from the stories of fantasy writer Ray Bradbury.

Bill also wanted to explore the topic of war in comics. The Korean War had broken out in 1950, and interest in combat comics was high. Bill hired a brilliant artist-writer named Harvey Kurtzman. His initial projects were two war comics, *Two-Fisted Tales* and *Frontline Combat*. Kurtzman's war comics were as daring and creative as anything else in the EC line. In a bold approach, he presented war in a harshly realistic light. Modern combat was shown to be horrible and often senseless, not glorious, as in many flag-waving World War II movies. Kurtzman even dared to write some of his stories from the enemy's point of view.

The Birth of MAD

By 1951, Bill was putting out nine comic books that were among the most popular in America. But Harvey Kurtzman was unhappy. Bill was paying him much less than Al Feldstein, because he was editing only two comics, as opposed to Feldstein's seven. Bill told Kurtzman that if he wanted a raise, he should come up with a new comic book—something totally devoted to humor. Kurtzman came up with a daring idea—a comic book that made fun of other comics.

In the summer of 1952, the first 32-page issue of *Tales Calculated to Drive You MAD* appeared on the newsstands. Kurtzman had chosen as his first targets four of EC's own comics. Bill thought it was great fun and loved Kurtzman's wild humor. The public, however, didn't agree, and the first issue didn't sell well. Another publisher might have dropped the new comic book. Bill, however, decided to support *MAD* a bit longer and see if it would find its audience.

3

The Rise of MAD

"We spare nothing to make each magazine, each story, each page, a work of art."

Comic books did not do well in 1954. In April, a well-known American psychiatrist (a doctor who deals with disorders of the mind), Fredric Wertham, published a book condemning comic books for leading America's innocent youth astray. Dr. Wertham claimed that comics drove youngsters to violence, crime, and even murder. At the top of his list of dangerous comics were those that dealt with crime and horror.

Comics Under Attack

That very same month in 1954, the Senate subcommittee on juvenile delinquency began hearings that looked into comic-book

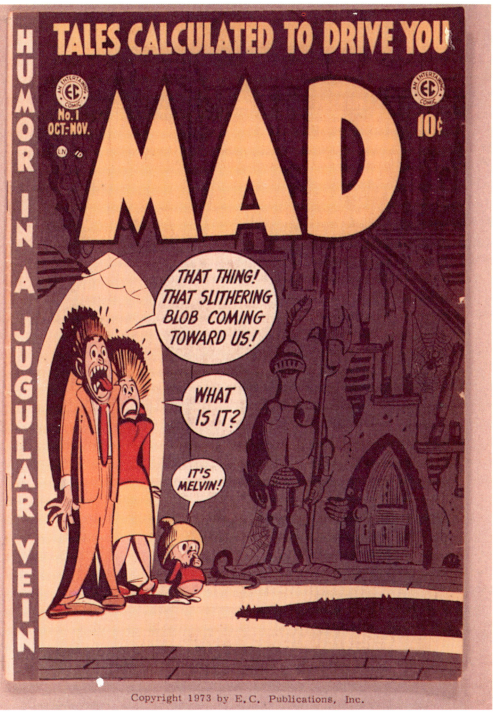

The first issue of MAD was launched in the summer of 1952. Though it got off to a rocky start, it soon became a great success nationwide.

violence. EC Comics were among the most criticized. Appearing before the subcommittee, Bill denied that his comics had a bad effect on their readers and defended them strongly. "I am proud of the comics I publish," he told the subcommittee. "We use the best writers, the finest artists; we spare nothing to make each magazine, each story, each page, a work of art...."

But where Bill saw art, some people saw "slime." Across the nation, churches and community groups staged comic-book burnings. Wholesalers refused to distribute the comic books in question, including EC's. To avoid any further trouble, comic-book publishers established the Comics Code Authority. This group called for the elimination of certain illustrations in comics. No monsters, except the classic Hollywood ones, could be used, and all authority figures had to be shown the greatest respect. The only comics that would reach the newsstands would be the ones with the code's seal of approval. Comic-book publisher Bill Gaines was obviously concerned.

Without a distributor, Bill was forced to discontinue EC's horror and crime comics. A later attempt to bring them back as paperbacks for adults failed. So did an EC line of

"squeaky clean" comics. *MAD* was about all
that remained of Bill's comic-book empire.

Bill decided to put all his money into
MAD. At Kurtzman's insistence, *MAD* was
transformed from a comic-book format to a
magazine by enlarging the size and using
better paper. This way, it wouldn't matter if
the Comic Codes Authority found something
in *MAD* it didn't like. *MAD* would no longer
be a comic book.

The New MAD

In the summer of 1955, *MAD*, the magazine,
appeared with an elaborate logo and fancy
border on its cover and a 25-cent price tag.
Among the writers in this issue was TV
funnyman Ernie Kovacs. Unlike the first
issue of the comic-book version, this *MAD*
was a big success.

Despite the magazine's success, EC was
in serious financial trouble because of the
loss of its other comics. Bill had to borrow
$50,000 from his mother just to keep the
business going. This time, when Kurtzman
demanded a controlling interest in the
magazine, Bill let him go. Al Feldstein took
over as *MAD*'s new editor.

Some readers felt that *MAD* lost its
special humor when Kurtzman left. While

Bill sits in his office in 1954, just before he released a newly designed version of MAD, which was an instant success.

Feldstein lacked Kurtzman's outrageous sense of humor, he did have a better feel for what people wanted. He widened the magazine's appeal by broadening its satire (humor that pokes fun at other things) to include all of American culture.

One of its first targets was the world of advertising. *MAD*'s takeoffs on ads were so deadly accurate that it was sometimes difficult to tell them from the originals.

MAD also began to poke fun at movies. The actors and movie plots were carefully followed, with lots of clever twists along the way. Over the years, nearly every box-office hit has received the *MAD* treatment, from *Flawrence of Arabia* (*Lawrence of Arabia*) to *Star Roars* (*Star Wars*).

Even great literature wasn't spared. Such classic American poems as Henry Wadsworth Longfellow's "Paul Revere's Ride" and Edgar Allan Poe's "The Raven" fell victim to *MAD*'s satire. Not a single word of the originals was changed—the humor was all in the outrageous illustrations that took every line literally. Later, *MAD* cleverly transformed other classics. The magazine published a "cool" beatnik version of Lincoln's Gettysburg Address and endless variations of Mother Goose nursery rhymes in different styles. These versions were so good that one educational publication actually praised *MAD* and recommended that teachers use it in the classroom to get their students interested in good literature. So much for Dr. Wertham's notion that comic books were leading America's youth astray!

Three MADmen

American social life became the specialty of the *MAD* artist-writer David Berg. His "The Lighter Side of..." series is one of the magazine's longest-running features. In it, Berg pokes gentle fun at every American institution from baseball to street crime.

Two of *MAD*'s most famous contributors, Don Martin and Antonio Prohías, are harder to classify. Don Martin, who left *MAD* in 1987, had been known as "*MAD*'s Maddest Artist." Over the years, Martin's flat-footed, long-faced characters and his unbelievably original sound effects had become a *MAD* trademark. In one classic comic, a customer checks into a hotel filled with cockroaches. He tries to call the desk clerk to complain, but the cockroaches lift him up and toss him out of the room. Downstairs he finds out that the desk clerk is a gigantic cigar-chomping cockroach!

Antonio Prohías, who was once Cuba's top political cartoonist, came to the United States in the early 1960s. He knew nothing about *MAD*, but decided that he wanted to work for the magazine because the name appealed to him. When he joined *MAD*, he developed the clever "Spy vs. Spy" feature. Prohías's Black Spy and White Spy have played their cat-and-mouse games in a seemingly endless number of variations. Occasionally, both of them are outsmarted by a third character, a gray female spy.

Alfred E. Neuman

Without a doubt, the best-known personality at *MAD* is the fictional "bad boy" and magazine mascot, Alfred E. Neuman. The character Alfred was originally called Melvin Coznowski. The crazy kid with the wide grin had a life long before *MAD*. He had been a favorite of artists for over a hundred years on postcards and in ads.

Wherever he came from, Alfred E. has become *MAD*'s number one MADman. He has appeared on nearly every cover of the magazine since 1955. And he has assumed the personality of everyone from Santa Claus to Alfredo, a pizza-eating Teenage Mutant Ninja Turtle.

By 1960, *MAD* magazine had made
Bill Gaines a multimillionaire and the
magazine's readership had exceeded one
million people. More than half of all college
students and more than 40 percent of all
high school students in the country were
reading *MAD* magazine. In 1961, on the
advice of his accountant, Bill sold *MAD*
magazine to Premier Industries, a manufac-
turer of venetian blinds. Bill stayed on as
publisher and retained almost total control
over the magazine. Working for Bill, many
staff members found out, could be both a
delightful and, at times, a "maddening"
experience.

4

Life at MAD

*"**MAD** was [Bill's] life's work, his hobby, his social life."*

Employers often like to think about their workers as part of one "big, happy family." At *MAD*, Bill Gaines carried this idea to an extreme. He showed his artists and writers that he really cared about them. He said goodbye to every single employee at the day's end and took them on wild and crazy vacations every year. But that same boss also refused to share copyrights to any work appearing in his magazine with artists and writers. He was very cost conscious and would sometimes spend hours, for example, hunting down a person who had made a personal call on an office phone.

Company-Paid Vacations

Some staff members at *MAD* had a "love-hate relationship" with their boss. "Bill has always had a very strong intellectual understanding of the democratic processes," Kurtzman once said. "Up to a certain point; then he turned into a monster."

Despite his occasional "monster" moods, Bill could be very kind. At *MAD*'s annual Christmas parties he would give out expensive presents. As the years went by, these presents became large bonuses, or money gifts. In 1960, Bill, who loved to travel, began taking his entire staff on free trips. Perhaps the most memorable moment of the 1960 *MAD* vacation to Haiti was when Bill discovered that there was only one person in Haiti who had a subscription to *MAD*, and his subscription was about to end. One afternoon, the entire staff hopped into rented jeeps and drove to the person's house. One can only imagine his surprise when he opened the door to find the publisher of *MAD*, surrounded by the "usual gang of idiots," handing him a gift subscription!

The staff vacation quickly became a yearly event. Bill led his workers on merry romps through Italy, Greece, Kenya, Hong Kong, London, Copenhagen, Leningrad,

Bill poses in his safari outfit. Company-paid vacations to exotic places were one of MAD's most popular fringe benefits for employees.

Bill is greeted by enthusiastic fans at London's Heathrow airport in 1971. MAD has enjoyed great popularity in many countries around the world.

Moscow, Amsterdam, and many other places. Wherever they went, Bill, a big man with a gigantic appetite, always sought out the best restaurants for serious feasting. Eating and lounging around were Bill's favorite activities on vacation. *MAD* artists spent their time sketching the local landscape and drawing caricatures (cartoon illustrations that exaggerate a person's physical features) of one another and their boss.

Work and Romance

Back home, life at *MAD* was a little more orderly. The offices of *MAD* are located, fittingly, at 485 MAD(ison) Avenue in New York City on the 13th floor. (Most office buildings have no 13th floor, because the number 13 is thought to be unlucky.)

The first thing that a visitor to the *MAD* offices sees is a life-size fake bronze statue of Alfred E. Neuman in military uniform. It stands opposite a Christmas tree that never comes down, (except during the Christmas season!). Down the hall is the office that Bill once occupied. It is a monument to the man's strange habits. Several model airships dangle from the ceiling and a human skull sits on the bookshelves. (Bill loved to tell visitors it was his father's.) Scattered on the floor are large stacks of papers and magazines. Next to the desk, believe it or not, hangs a life-size picture of the back of Bill Gaines's head.

Bill himself was just the opposite of the typical self-made man. Bill had first started his publishing career as a young, clean-cut executive. As he became more successful, however, he grew a beard, let his hair grow to shoulder length, and started wearing baggy pants and old shirts to work. He encouraged his employees to dress in a casual way, too. "He became uncomfortable if people started to wear shirts and ties and pinstripe suits," recalled long-time friend and *MAD*man Nick Meglin, "because he figured they were looking to become corporate creeps, as he would call them."

"*MAD* was his life's work, his hobby, his social life," Meglin said. The magazine also led Bill to his last two wives. In 1955, he married Nancy Siegel, who worked in *MAD*'s subscription department. Bill and Nancy had three children, but divorced in 1971. The events that led Bill to meet his third wife were unexpected and a little more complicated.

In 1970, a college student in Pennsylvania named Anne Griffiths wrote to Bill,

Bill stops for a rest during a company-paid vacation to Holland in 1971.

requesting a *MAD* article for a paper she was writing for one of her courses. Anne's sense of humor and personality appealed to Bill. Soon after, while on a trip to Pennsylvania, he stopped by to say hello. After the two had dinner, they continued writing to

Bill always counted himself lucky for being able to run a successful business and have fun at the same time.

each other. After transferring to the University of Colorado, Anne went to New York to study art. By the time she had graduated, she was living with Bill there. She started working at *MAD* in 1980, and the two were wed seven years later.

Bill Gaines had a lot of fun running *MAD*, with little interference from Warner Communications, the company that had taken over the magazine in 1969. He had made the magazine the success it was, and Warner saw no reason to change it. What is the secret of that success? It may come as a surprise to many of *MAD*'s most devoted fans that, under that long gray hair, lurked the mind of a very insightful and shrewd businessman.

Bill and Anne had a long-time friendship before they were married in 1987.

5

A "MAD" Genius

"We really publish **MAD** *to please ourselves."*

"We've always taken the position that we don't care who reads *MAD*," Bill Gaines once said. "We really publish *MAD* to please ourselves. It isn't very businesslike, but it's the way I do it."

Breaking All the Rules

The way Bill "did it" was to break just about every rule of magazine publishing. Unlike other magazines, *MAD* has never conducted a survey to see who their readers are. *MAD* also didn't work very hard at obtaining subscribers. A one-year subscription saves the reader about a quarter off the cover price. And *MAD* takes in no advertising on its

Bill always managed to keep a sense of humor no matter what he was doing.

Bill poses with MAD artist Jack Davis during a vacation. MAD's exceptionally talented artists were one of the keys to its success.

pages. Bill said he never wanted to risk offending any advertisers, a good point when you consider the magazine's history of poking fun at the ad business. But there's more to it than that. Bill knew that advertisers would insist he upgrade the cheap newsprint to expensive, slick magazine paper, and he wasn't about to do that.

Perhaps strangest of all, *MAD* didn't advertise itself either—neither in ads nor in the use of the *MAD* name on other products. Since *MAD* makes fun of people who try to sell themselves, Bill didn't think it was right to do that. However, there have been a few products that carry the *MAD* name, some of them very successful. The *MAD* board game, for example, has sold 3 million copies.

A large statue of Alfred E. Neuman stands in the offices of MAD as a constant inspiration to be crazy.

A Master of Repackaging

So how did Bill make *MAD* the success it has been for more than 40 years? One of the secrets is repackaging. Since the appearance of *The MAD Reader* in 1954, *MAD* has put together nearly 100 paperbacks containing old material from the magazine. There have been more than 100 other paperbacks of original work by some of *MAD's* best-known writers and artists that Bill also made money on. Each year, *MAD* also produces four large "super specials" and two collector's series special issues that sell for $3.50 and contain material going back to *MAD's* comic-book days. All these reprints have been profitable.

Bill never threw anything away. Back in the early days of EC, he saved all the original art from his comics. He figured that one day they would be worth something. Now, with comic-book art a respectable part of popular culture, these comic-book covers and panels sell for thousands of dollars. EC comics are considered classics. In the 1980s, all Bill's horror, sci-fi, and war comics were reprinted in handsome hardcover collectors' volumes.

Bill also knew just how his creations should be adapted to other popular forms of

In 1985, Bill and EC comics were inducted into the Horror Hall of Fame. Bill regarded that honor as one of the highlights of his life.

entertainment. The *MAD Show* was an off-Broadway musical hit in 1965, and ran for over two years. HBO's series *Tales from the Crypt*, based on the EC horror comic, has been HBO's most successful series since its first show in 1989. It even brought back the comic's Crypt-Keeper as a remarkably life-like puppet.

MAD Today

MAD itself is no longer the hit it was back in the early 1970s, when circulation reached two and a half million a year. The magazine, however, still has plenty of life left in it. There are 11 foreign-language editions of *MAD*. The German edition has the largest circulation of any humor magazine in Europe.

In 1984, Al Feldstein finally retired as editor. Nick Meglin and John Ficarra, two long-time *MAD* associate editors, became the magazine's co-editors. But Bill remained in charge right up till the end. Nearing his seventieth birthday he declared, "I do not plan to retire, ever. Either I'll die here in my chair, or they'll fire me." He died on June 3, 1992, not in his chair, but barely out of it, after a brief illness.

Bill Gaines will be remembered fondly by several generations of young people, many of whom are now adults. In his EC comics he took what some people considered trash and turned it into art. In *MAD* he taught us that not only can humor make us laugh, which is good, but it can also make us *think*, which is better.

"What's amazing about *MAD* is how long it's lasted," writes magazine consultant James Kobak. "It's hard to keep a humor

Bill's office—filled with a clutter of cartoons and comics—was one of his favorite places.

magazine fresh. Most tend to outlive their audiences, and then they die."

But over the years *MAD* has become more than just a magazine. It has become a part of America's cultural heritage. And somewhere William M. Gaines is smiling with a big "Alfred E." grin. What—Me Worry? Not a chance.

Glossary

adaptation A work of literature that is changed to another format.

circulation Number of magazine copies that are distributed and sold.

copyright The legal right granted to one person or company to publish and sell a book or a musical or artistic work.

logo A company's identifying symbol.

mascot A person, animal, or object adopted by a group as a symbolic figure.

satire Humor that pokes fun at a person, a thing, or an institution.

subscription An advance purchase of a publication for a specified period of time.

trademark A word or a symbol that identifies an original product.

For Further Reading

Crawford, Hubert H. *Crawford's Encyclopedia of Comic Books*. Middle Village, NY: Jonathan David, 1978.

Jacob, Frank. *The MAD World of William M. Gaines*. New York: Bantam Books, 1973.

Reidelbach, Maria. *Completely MAD: A History of the Comic Book and Magazine*. Boston: Little Brown & Company, 1991.

Wertham, Fredric. *Seduction of the Innocent*. New York: Rinehart, 1954.

Index

Photo Credits:
Cover: Courtesy of Anne Gaines.
Pp. 4, 7, 10, 11, 12, 15, 31, 35, 37, 39, 40, 43, 45: Courtesy of Anne Gaines; p. 17: *Tales from the Crypt*, Feb.–March. 1951–vol.1, No. 22 ©1950 by I.C. Publishing Co., Inc. re ©1978 by William M. Gaines. Used with permission from William P. Gaines, Agent, Inc.; p. 21: ©1952, 1980 by E.C. Publications, Inc.; p. 24, 32, 36, 41: Wide World Photos.